Scarlett the Cat
to the Rescue
Fire Hero

by Nancy Loewen

illustrated by Kristin Sorra

PICTURE WINDOW BOOKS
a capstone imprint

March 29, 1996
Brooklyn, New York

East New York was a troubled neighborhood. Rundown buildings and trash-filled lots were all around. Amidst falling snow the broken city landscape was cold and wet.

In this grim setting, a young cat became a hero to people around the world.

2

Just before dawn, in an
abandoned garage, a young
mama cat curled up with her
five kittens. The cat was thin
and cold. Still, she purred as
her kittens nursed.

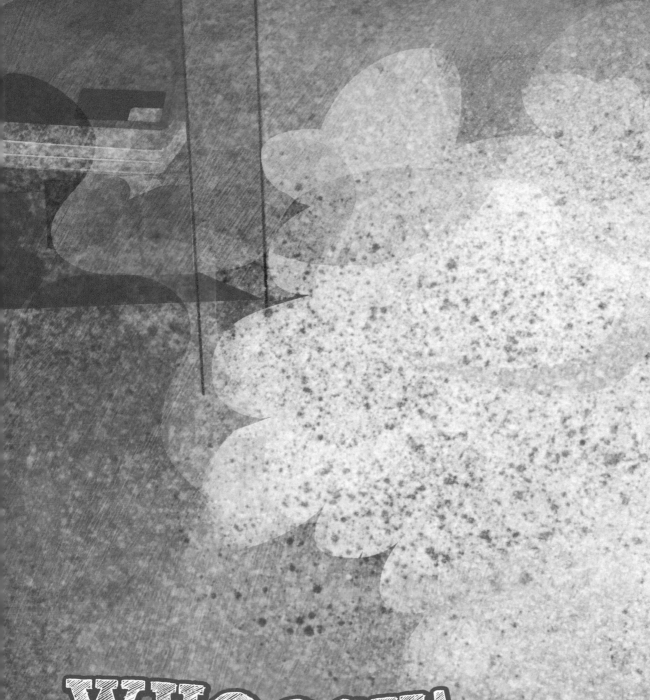

WHOOSH!

What was that sound? Crackling flames appeared in the corner. A sharp, stinging smell filled the air. The mama cat crouched over her kittens. A low growl filled her throat.

The mama cat was used to protecting herself from stray dogs and cats and sometimes even mean kids who threw rocks. But this enemy was different. There was nothing to scratch or bite. The danger was all around.

Her kittens—she had to get them out!
Roughly she picked up the closest one by the
scruff of its neck and ran with it out of the
garage. She dropped the kitten at the side of
the building next door.

Then she ran like a streak
back into the smoke and flames.

Out on the street, sirens blared. Soon
the area was filled with firefighters and
bystanders. No one noticed when a skinny
cat with singed ears dropped off a second
kitten...and then went back for another...and
another...and another.

When the fire was under control,
a firefighter named David Giannelli
heard a sound he wasn't expecting.

He looked around, listening hard.
There they were! Three tiny kittens!

Mew!
Mew!
Mew!

David put the kittens safely into a box. Then he found another kitten at the curb—and one more on the ground a few yards away.

David figured that the kittens must have been carried out of the burning building by their mother. And what a mother she was! David had a lot of experience rescuing animals. He knew that when cats are faced with fire, they usually hide for as long as they can. At the last moment, they make a mad dash for safety.

But this cat had gone into a burning building, over and over again!

David began searching for the mama cat.
Finally he found her across the street, in a
vacant lot. Her eyes were blistered shut. Her face
was mostly bare skin. Her paws were badly burned.
Large patches of fur had been singed off her
body. She was barely alive.

Carefully, David placed the cat in the box
with her kittens. Though the mama cat couldn't
see, she touched each one of her babies with
her nose. It was as if she was counting them
to make sure they were all there.

David drove the cat and her kittens through the snowy streets to the North Shore Animal League in Port Washington, New York.

The staff was ready and waiting. They gave the cats fluids and medicine and put salve on burned skin. Then they put the entire cat family into a special tent filled with oxygen. The cats' lungs had been hurt by smoke, and the oxygen would help them breathe.

As a stray, the mama cat probably hadn't been around
people very much. Yet she seemed to trust the staff to take
care of her and her kittens.

Very soon, the brave mama cat received a name: Scarlett.
She was named after the determined main character in the
Civil War story, *Gone with the Wind*.

The news of Scarlett's courage spread quickly. That very morning local reporters and photographers filled the clinic. Then the story went out into the city, nation, and even the world! People everywhere were inspired by what this young street cat had done for her kittens.

Scarlett lived at the clinic for three months
as her injuries healed. She loved attention.
And everyone loved her.

The kittens moved to a foster home but came back a couple of times to visit their mother. One kitten, a white one named Toasty, died from a virus about a month after the fire. Two of the other kittens became sick, too, but they got better.

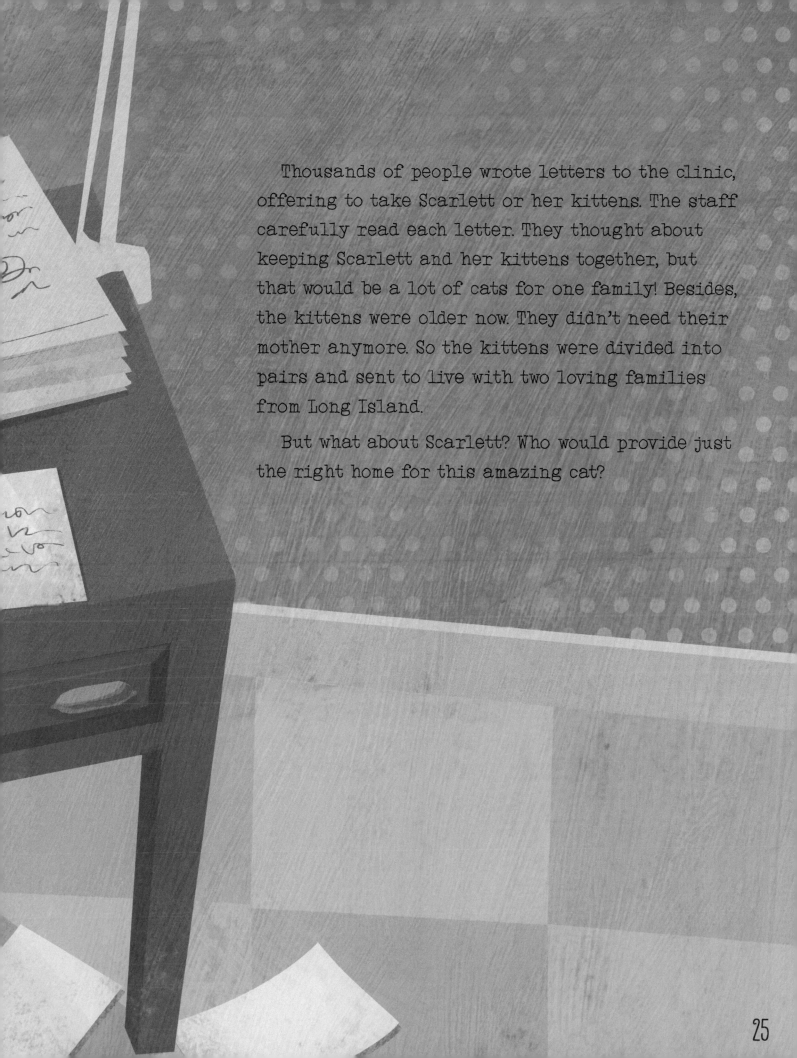

Thousands of people wrote letters to the clinic, offering to take Scarlett or her kittens. The staff carefully read each letter. They thought about keeping Scarlett and her kittens together, but that would be a lot of cats for one family! Besides, the kittens were older now. They didn't need their mother anymore. So the kittens were divided into pairs and sent to live with two loving families from Long Island.

But what about Scarlett? Who would provide just the right home for this amazing cat?

One day the staff read a letter from a woman named Karen Wellen.

Karen lived with her parents in their roomy three-story home in Brooklyn. Someone would always be around to care for Scarlett. That was important, because Scarlett would need eye drops every day for the rest of her life.

Karen wrote that after losing her own cat and
being hurt in a car accident, she'd become a more
caring person. If she ever got another cat, she
wanted it to be one with special needs.

It was the perfect match.

The skinny cat who used to search for food in the streets now had regular meals. She had plenty of soft places to sleep and windows that let in the light. She had three people to give her all the love she deserved.

And every day Karen's mother sang a well-known song to Scarlett. It was called, "You Are So Beautiful."

The rest of the world would agree!

Afterword

Scarlett's story was covered by CNN, PBS, CBS, Animal Planet, Oprah Winfrey, and even news organizations as far away as Germany and Japan. Years later, people were still interested in hearing updates about Scarlett and her four surviving kittens (Oreo, Cinders, Tanuki, and Samsara). Scarlett had many health problems, but she remained active and loving her whole life. Her favorite game was to run through tunnels made from paper bags. She died in 2008 at the age of 13.

But no one is likely to forget about Scarlett any time soon. The North Shore Animal League created the "Scarlett Award for Animal Heroism" in Scarlett's honor. And she even has a Facebook page ("Scarlett the cat") with thousands of "likes."

Glossary

abandoned—deserted or neglected; empty

bystander—a person who watches something but doesn't take part

foster home—a safe home where pets can live for a short time; pets sometimes stay in foster homes before they are adopted

grim—sad, gloomy

salve—a thick medicine that is applied to skin

scruff—the back of the neck

singe—to burn or scorch

staff—people who work at a certain place; employees

temporary—short-term, not permanent

Read More

125 True Stories of Amazing Animals. National Geographic Kids. Washington, D.C.: National Geographic, 2012.

Driscoll, Laura. *The Bravest Cat!: The True Story of Scarlett*. New York: Grosset & Dunlap, 1997.

Spinelli, Eileen. *Hero Cat*. New York: Two Lions, 2011.

Critical Thinking with the Common Core

The firefighter who discovered the kittens, and who later found Scarlett, knew that Scarlett was a very special cat. Why was Scarlett's behavior considered so unusal? *(Key Ideas and Details)*

Look at these words on page 5: "WHOOSH! What was that sound?" "Whoosh" isn't a word that is used very often. How does it make you feel? How do the capital letters and exclamation point add to its effect? In the sentence that follows, from whose point of view are we seeing the action? *(Craft and Structure)*

After the fire, Scarlett needed eye drops three times a day. Think of all the pets you know—your own and those of friends and family. Do any of them have health problems that need special care? What are the challenges and rewards of taking care of such an animal? *(Integration of Knowledge and Ideas)*

Internet Sites

FactHound offers a safe, fun way to find Internet sites related to this book. All of the sites on FactHound have been researched by our staff.

Here's all you do:

Visit *www.facthound.com*

Type in this code: 9781479554645

Super-cool stuff! Check out projects, games and lots more at **www.capstonekids.com**

Editor: Jeni Wittrock
Designer: Ashlee Suker
Art Director: Nathan Gassman
Production Specialist: Tori Abraham
The illustrations in this book were created digitally.

Picture Window Books are published by Capstone,
1710 Roe Crest Drive, North Mankato, Minnesota 56003
www.capstonepub.com

Library of Congress Cataloging-in-Publication Data
Loewen, Nancy, 1964–
Scarlett the Cat to the Rescue: Fire Hero/by Nancy Loewen; illustrated by Kristin Sorra.
pages cm.—(Nonfiction Picture Books. Animal Heroes)
Includes bibliographical references.
Summary: "Simple text and full-color illustrations describe the true story of Scarlett, the stray
cat that famously saved her kittens from a Brooklyn garage fire"—Provided by publisher.
ISBN 978-1-4795-5464-5 (library binding)
SBN 978-1-4795-5468-3 (paperback)
ISBN 978-1-4795-5762-2 (paper over board)
ISBN 978-1-4795-5472-0 (ebook pdf)
1. Scarlett (Cat)—Juvenile literature. 2. Cats—New York (State)—New York—Juvenile
literature. I. Title.
SF445.7.L64 2015
636.8—dc23   2014011381

Photo Credit: Getty Images/Time & Life Pictures/Taro Yamasaki, 29

Look for all the books in the series:

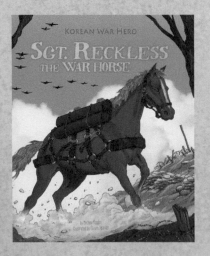

Printed in the United States   5469